Mel Bay's Gypsy Violin

by Mary Ann Harbar

Would you like to know how to move your audience to tears, or compel them to leap to their feet in thrilled applause? For centuries these closely guarded secrets of Gypsy violininsts have been handed down from one generation to the next. Now, you too can command your instrument's expressive powers with Gyspy Violin.

Contents

Visit us on the Web at www.melbay.com — E-mail us at email@melbay.com

2 3 4 5 6 7 8 9 0

How to Use this Book

As you read this book you'll encounter terms, including those **bold and italicized** in the text, both new and familiar. Many denote the numerous articulations and other devices that give this music its appealing passion, variety, and contrast in texture, timbre, dynamics, and tempo. Look them up in the **Glossary** to learn how you can transform your playing into sheer enchantment!

Table of Contents

The Gypsy Touch

Gypsies have swift, typically uncalloused fingers and a light touch with both hands. Feel the sensation of the strings with your left fingerpads. The fleshy portion of the finger is employed in *Gypsy Violin* to execute all manner of slides, vibrato, trills, and grace notes. The cobra-like left-hand finger action in fast passages emphasizes the reflexive release more than the strike.

The fingers of the bow hand are flexible and the bow hair loose. Feel the bow hair against the string through your right-hand fingers. Try twisting your wrist counterclockwise to minimize the participation of all but the index (and second) finger(s). Additionally, you can hold the bow close to the fingertips for dexterity, and play on the edge of the hair.

The default *prímás* and *harmony* bowstroke ( ) has more separation between the notes than the singing, classical detaché or the fiddle sawstroke. Combine the *detaché porté* with the *semi-staccato* to produce rhythmic articulation. Almost stop the bow between the notes. Sometimes eighth and quarter notes have a dotted feel as well. Bowings and articulations are listed at the beginning of the Glossary.

See *kontra* and *bass* in the Glossary for their bowing styles.

Practice Tips

Listen to the music before you play it, to establish it firmly in your mind. It has many unusual qualities. In addition to the companion CD for this book, Gypsy CDs from Europe are now available in America.

Intersperse your practicing with other activities throughout the day to alternately exercise and relax new muscles.

Practice with others as often as possible. Practice the songs, particularly trouble spots, *a tempo,* in sections.

Practice *friss* passages in dotted rhythms for clarity, placing unintentionally "swallowed" notes on the long stroke of the dotted pair.

Practice holding long notes 30 counts to a bow for control in passages.

Control your bow distribution, particularly on the slow numbers, by following the given bowings or basing your own on the same principle. Fast notes can take advantage of the facility of the upper half of the bow, accented or loud notes of the weight at the frog, and long notes with *crescendo* often use an upbow to take advantage of increased power approaching the frog.

Use the fingerings herein, designed for agility or expression, or create your own with these attributes in mind.

This music was created by violinists to lie naturally under the fingers and bow. Use your imagination to customize the music to your taste.

The Violin

Gypsy violinists often prefer an instrument with a dark sound.

Without a violin shop handy, they often do their own instrument maintenance and repair. They loop a piece of string around the soundpost to move it around, and shape the bridge with sandpaper. Low action is generally preferred to facilitate fast fingerings. The bridge is re-notched to place strings wider apart to accommodate large hands.

Oils from the skin (and from food!) can lubricate the fingerboard and facilitate shifts and slides. Alternately, you can use a dab of vegetable oil, which is also used to polish the instrument and bow stick. A mild lanolin-free liquid detergent is used on dirty bow hair.

About the Recordings

We recorded these tunes in a variety of ways to give you an idea of the endless possibilities for playing them. Repeats were sometimes omitted so we could include all the songs on the CD. You will hear *codas* that aren't in the book on many tunes. These can be improvised. (*See "coda"* in the Glossary.)

Acknowledgments

I am indebted to my fellow musicians whose unique and outstanding talents you hear on the available CD.

Greg Harbar, of Byelorussian descent and leader for 20 years of our Houston-based ethnic strolling and dance band *The Gypsies*, plays accordion. He also helped write and edit the music in this volume.

David Klingensmith, B.A. in Music from Rice University, and very active teacher and performer in jazz, orchestral and rock music, and shows, plays upright bass.

Zhenya Kolykhanov, from Moscow with a background in Russian theatre and folk as well as rock music, currently tours with the Russian group *Red Elvis*. He illustrated this volume and plays guitar on the Russian tunes.

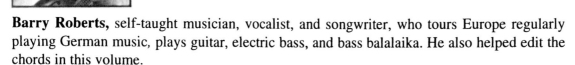

Kelly Lancaster, from Nacogdoches, Texas and winner of guitar and mandolin contests nationwide (as well as working with Willie Nelson and numerous other bands), plays guitar, bass balalaika, and mandobass. He also helped edit the chords in this volume. His instructional video *Gypsy Jazz Guitar* is available through Mel Bay Publications.

Dave Peters, the only three-time national champion, who works with his bluegrass, new acoustic and jazz ensemble in Japan, Switzerland, and the U.S., plays mandolin.

Barry Roberts, self-taught musician, vocalist, and songwriter, who tours Europe regularly playing German music, plays guitar, electric bass, and bass balalaika. He also helped edit the chords in this volume.

Alexis Valk, D.A. in Music, and former Commercial Music Department Head at Houston Community College as well as instructor, clinician, and performer in jazz, plays upright bass.

Dedication

To my husband Greg Harbar, musician and ethnomusicologist, whose enthusiasm inspired this book.

His personal wealth of knowledge and experience, vast sheet music and recording library, and network of colleagues, provided the material for this publication. I am grateful for his selfless dedication and contribution to ethnic music.

Special thanks to the many others who generously contributed to this project. To name a few:

Ethnomusilogical consultation and instruction:

Hungarian Gypsy violinists **Istvan ("Pista" "Sisák") Farkas & Greg Ballog**
Romanian violinists **George Caba & Miamon Miller**

Greg Harbar
Michael Stillman, *Monitor Records*
Steve Wolownick

Instruments and equipment:
Gold Violin Shop
Suretone Products
Violin Gallery

Recording and mixdown:
Karl Caillouet
Dave Peters

Artwork:
Zhenya Kolykhanov

Photography:
Rick Gardner Photography

Translation:
Zoya Griffin
Olga Nitescu
Miklos Olah

A Minor-Universal Gypsy Tunes

The Basso

"The Basso" is actually composed by Gypsies and features the basic Gypsy *chord* progression IVm-Im-V-Im. We had the pleasure of recording this number with Singing Sam, an American Gypsy singer who was popular among Gypsies in this country before his untimely death a few a years ago. Section B features his alternate major *changes.* At the numerous Mačvaja, Kalderaš, and Boyash *slavas* we've participated in, this has been the dance tune of choice.

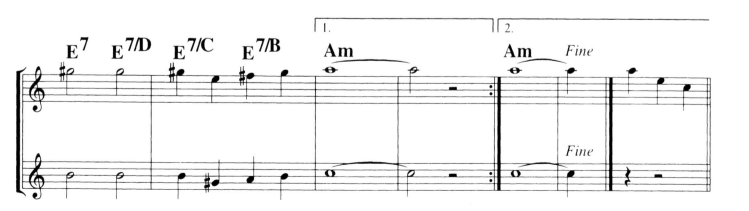

Kinokio

This authentic Gypsy gem could be Hungarian or Romanian. Start slow and gradually accelerate throughout the song and all repetitions.

A Minor-Russian Tunes

Turquoise Bracelets

Start this Russian Gypsy song " <u>Бирюзовые колечки</u> " ("Beryuzoviye Kalyechke") slowly and gradually *accelerate* over several verses.

My Gypsy Girl

Russian Gypsies have popularized this song "Мои Цыганочки" ("Moye Tziganochki"), with vocals and seven-string guitar. Start the tune slowly, picking up speed to the fifth bar. Play deliberately the final four bars of the coda with pickup.

Kalinka

The internationally popular " <u>Калинка</u> " is about a small winter-blooming tree with bright orange berries. Start slowly and play A with its first ending as many times as you like, ***accelerating*** each time and taking the second ending when you go to B. Play B twice at ***medium tempo,*** then play A1 the same way as A. The song can go on and on this way, the idea being to get everybody clapping and having a good time. Play the final second ending ***deliberately*** with a definite ***cutoff.***

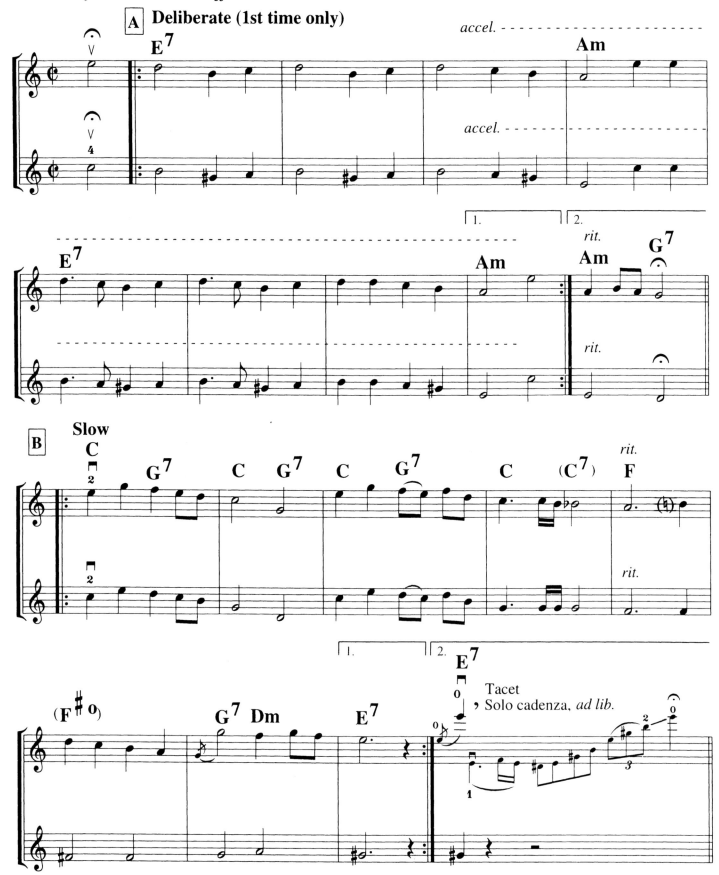

D Minor-Russian Tunes

Dark Eyes

This Russian Gypsy waltz, "Очи Черные" ("Otchi Tchornyia"), expounds rhapsodically about a girl's deep black, glistening eyes. This is a great tune for *improvising* at various tempi, and even in 4/4; use your imagination! We recorded it with the guitar taking the melody *rubato ad lib* once through before the violin enters at waltz tempo. He also played a G minor-D minor *arpeggiated cadenza* for a coda.

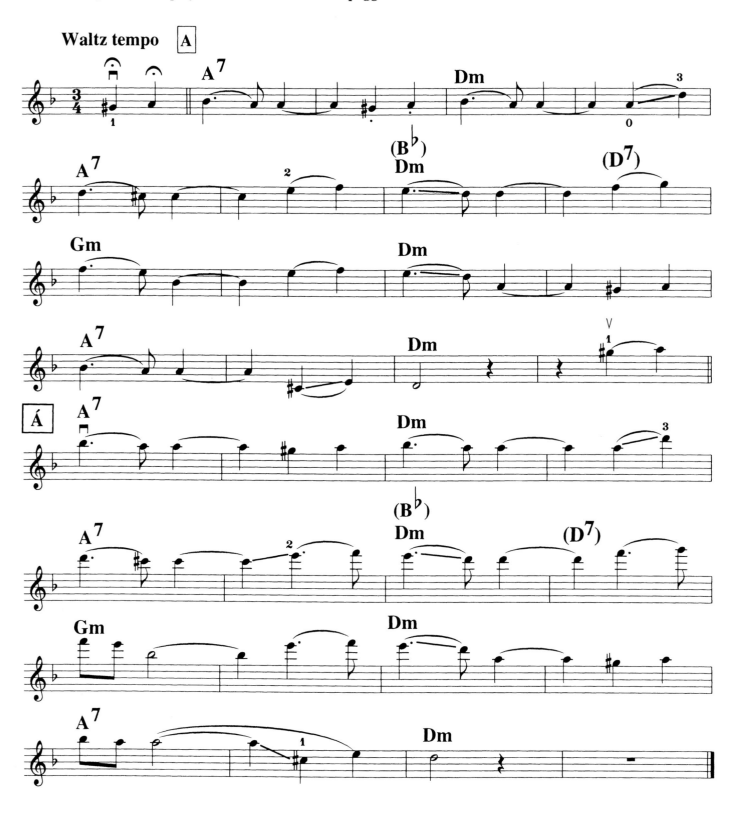

Two Guitars

This old Russian Gypsy song, " <u>Две Гнтары</u> " ("Dve Guitari"), reminisces about the good times of youth in a nightclub where two guitars serenaded the customers. Here we present a typical arrangement. Probably the most widely recognized Russian Gypsy tune, "Two Guitars" has been popularized worldwide, along with "Dark Eyes," a Russian favorite with Gypsies.

Medium tempo

G Minor/G Major-Romanian Tunes

Hora from Bucovina

"Hora Bucovinei" is a *joc* from this Romanian-influenced section of the Ukraine. The *Fraigish* scale, replete with *leading tones* gives it a *klezmer* sound. The extensive use of second position in the harmony part facilitates the trills to match those in the melody.

21

G Major Hora

Play the eighth note pickups almost like *grace notes.* Note the A♭ in section B, bar three, versus the A♮ in the repeat at bar nine; likewise the corresponding F and F♯ in the harmony part. Also, the harmony plays B♭ in the following bar four and B♮ in bar 10. *Rhythm section,* note the B section stops. An odd number of measures (7 x 2), characteristic of many Romanian *horas,* is found in the 14-bar B section.

22

D Minor/D Major-Romanian and Bessarabian Tunes

I Like Dances from Şomlecan

Compare the Hungarian Gypsy *changes* in this Transylvanian folk tune "Drag Mi Jocul Şomlecan", to the originals (written above each *chord*). The triplet near the end of each section is another Gypsy embellishment.

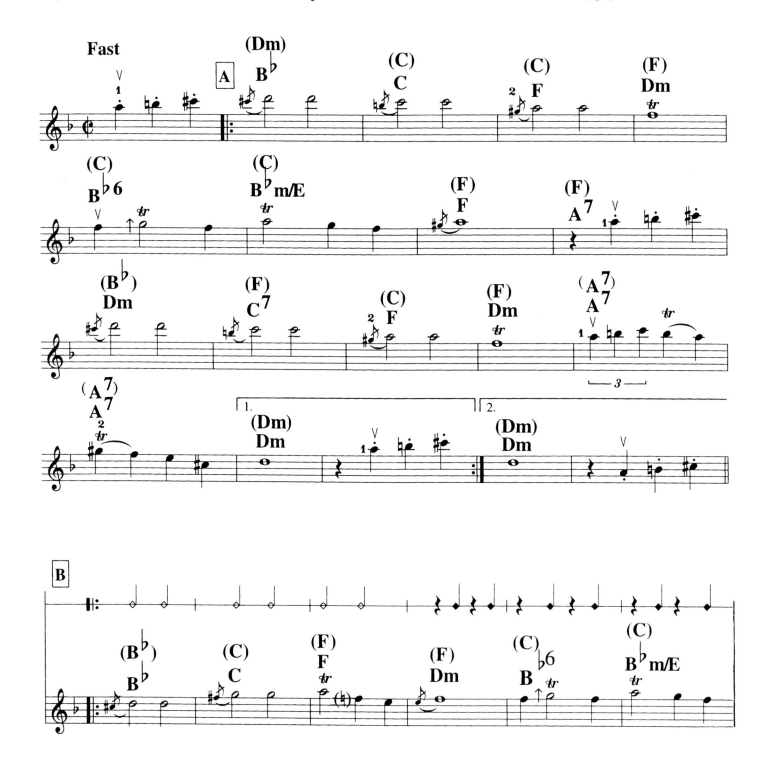

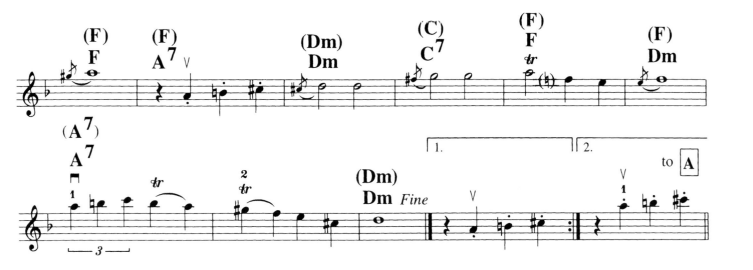

D Major Hora

Play the quarter notes in this lively "chaser" with a *dotted* feel.

Bessarabian Girl

In this number "Bessarabyanka" the first two lines of A and B respectively, constitute a hora from Bessarbia/Moldavia (formerly Romanian and Russian regions). Variations were added and a *doina* section sandwiched between the verses.

We start off at a half note = mm 190 or so, slowing down to around 132 in the middle section and resuming original tempo at bar five of D. A´ creates a variation using **pedal tones.** A second instrument can play the opening melody under this or the other variation starting at bar 17 of A and/or A´.

The exotic *doina* section features the **Romanian minor** scale, **sul G** and **D** passages, **sul ponticello** over a G minor **walking bass line,** and plenty of long notes where you can use the Gypsy **crescendo.** A Gypsy **prímás** holds those notes as long as he wishes and the rest of the ensemble follows him, the **cimbalom** embellishing with fills. We've packaged it into a straightforward version that your **bass** and **rhythm section** can count.

Sit on the starting note of the opening **slide** of this section, then take your time progressing to the target note.

28

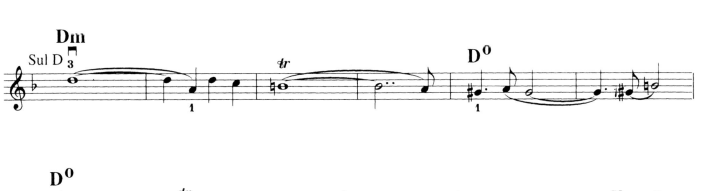

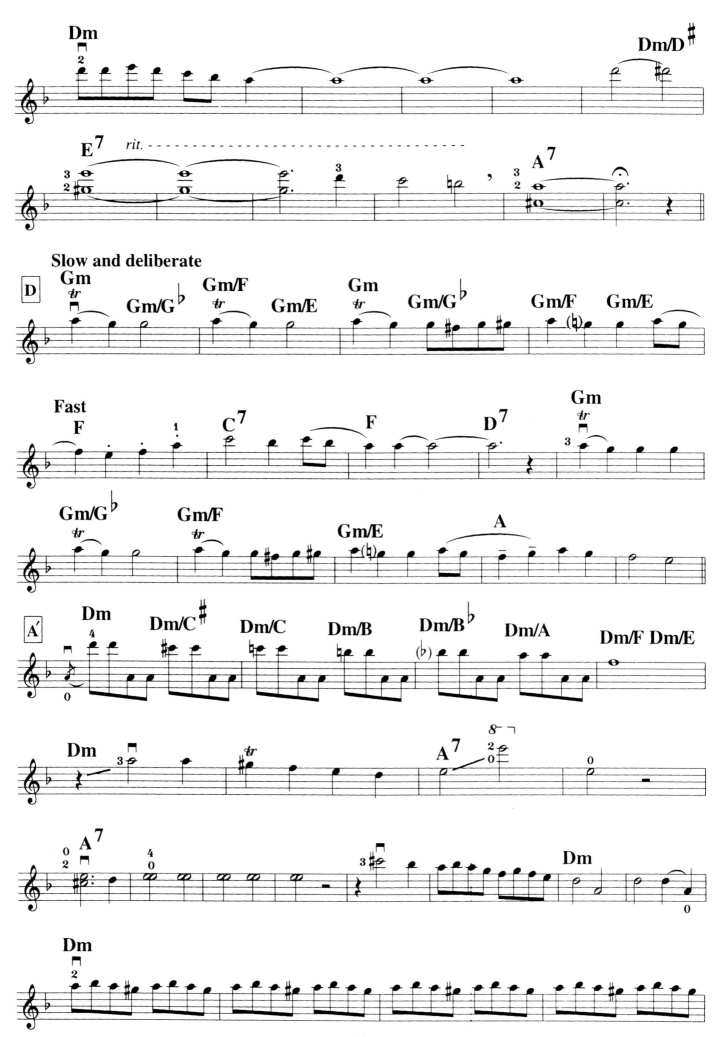

E Minor-Romanian Medley #1

Kamnes

After the *rubato* intro, this number kicks into a brisk clip, breaking tempo for the stately section B. The high E string "whistle" is the song's signature. Note the variation on this, *sliding* up to the high E harmonic and then back down from it on the reverse bow, like a "chirp." **Bass** and **rhythm** play one downbeat and one offbeat to the bar in B, which goes into 4/4 time (twice as slow as A). Revert to cut time where indicated and for the repeat of A.

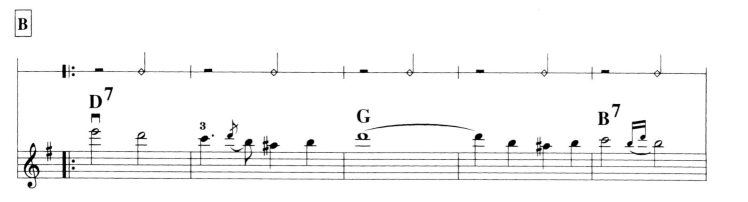

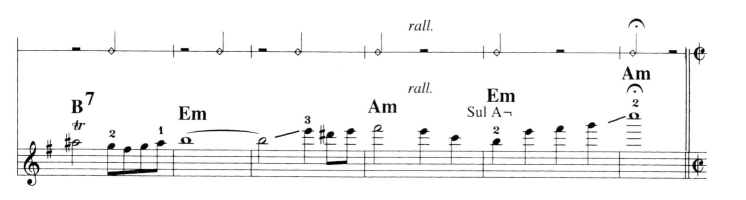

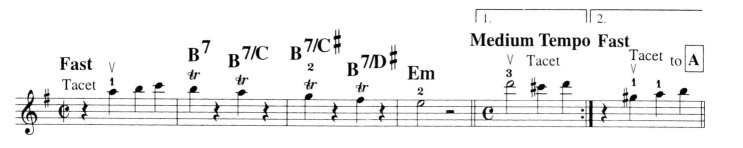

35

Whistling Hora

An abbreviated *doina* section would often be inserted into the middle of a Romanian *hora* such as this "Füttyhora." In this Hungarian Gypsy version, however, the added middle section increases tempo, while featuring the flashy *pedal tone* we've dubbed the "Kalisky riff." Play the idiomatic Hungarian *dotted* rhythm first appearing in bar two with a short, accented eighth note. The harmony C in bar 12 of section B may be *trilled* with the lower finger, B.

E Minor-Romanian Medley #2

Moldavian Hora

*This is a **joc** from Moldavia.*

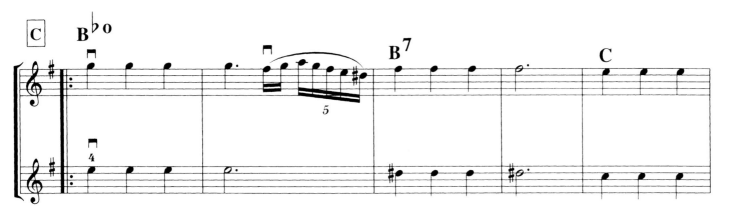

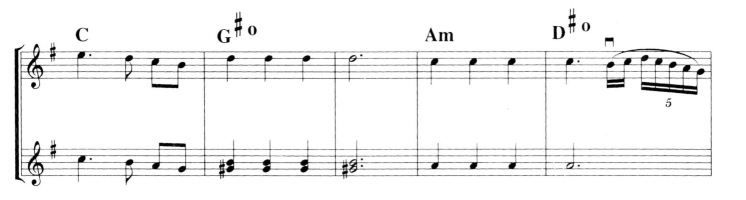

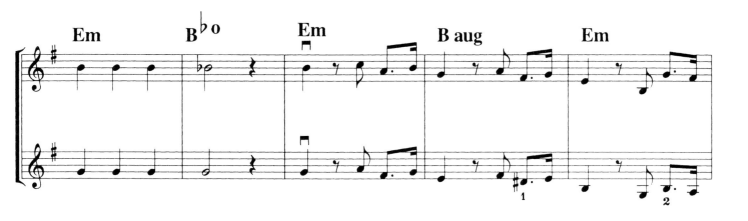

Romanian Train Song

We dubbed this the "Romanian 'Orange Blossom Special'" after its American counterpart. In section A, do a *left-hand pizzicato* on the open E while bowing on the D string. A second melody instrument can echo the first and third bars of B (plus their following downbeats), over the second and fourth bars.

B Minor-Romanian Tunes

B Minor Hora

The bass can do a chromatic rundown from B (B, B♭, A, G♯) four times during the introductory vamp. The *doina* section (C and C′) maintains the same tempo as the preceding verse. Speed up at D if you dare!

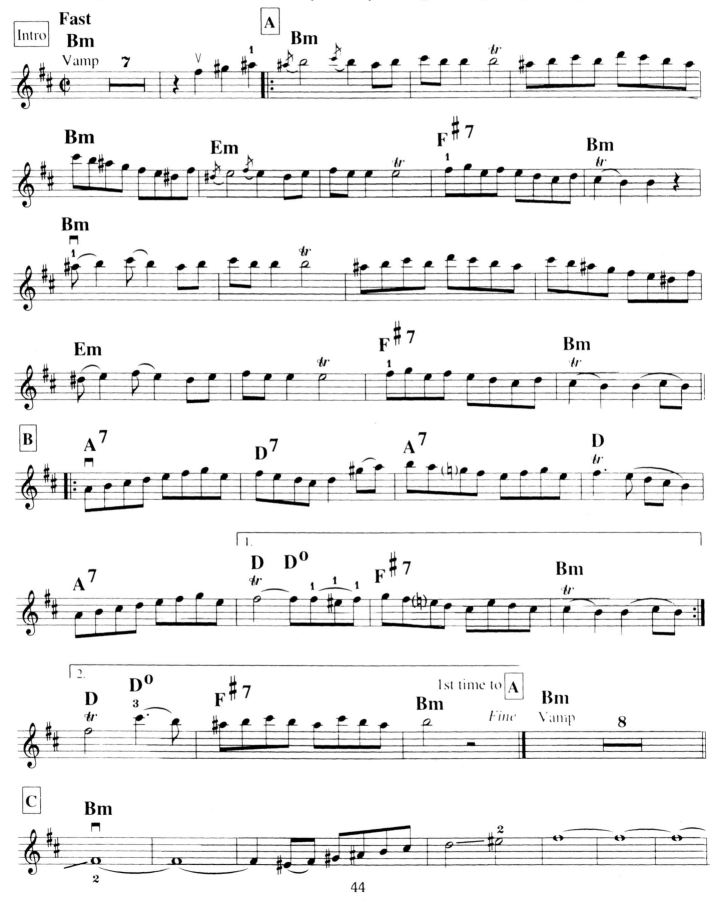

44

45

Cigarettes

Hungarian Gypsies created this fast hora from the Russian Jewish street song "Papirossen," about a cold and lonely orphan selling cigarettes on the street corner. Note the harmonization of the C and D sections, the walking bass line over the long E° in sections A and B, and the rhythm stops in section C. We play this with the format: AABBCCDDCAB.

7/8-Romanian Tune

Doda

Count this Romanian 7/8 tune "Dear Aunt" **1-2-3 1-2 1-2** (♩. ♩ ♩). You can play the trilled F's slightly sharp, trilling with the half step above. The G in bars four and 12 can also lean to the sharp side. Use the ***portato bowing*** in bars 7, 8, and 15.

F♯ Minor-Romanian Tune

March Hora

This showy *fast* number is named "Hora Marţişorŭlui" after little brightly colored ribbon lapel decorations Romanians exchange during their spring festival in March. Not for the faint of heart, it moves along at a brisk tempo.

Unusual rhythms and *changes* give this tune an eccentric quality. Sections B and D contain 5- and 10- bar phrases, respectively. Rhythm players, note the accented, syncopated stops in B, and the tricky progression here and in section C.

Bass players, note the *walking bass lines* in sections A and C, and *leading tones* including the raised fourth (C) in section C, bar three. Check the tritone drops in section D!

The song goes through four scalar permutations, beginning with the predominantly *harmonic minor* form of F♯. Section B switches to A major. Note the *leading tones* to the third (B♯ to C♯) and fifth (D♯ to E). Section C uses the F♯ *Romanian minor* scale. Section D is in A major, its melody punctuated by the D♯ *tritone.*

Use the *sautillé* bowing throughout, except on the D section melody.

Watch for tricky *leading tones* throughout, resulting in raised fingerings where you might not expect them. Hear them in your head before playing.

In section A, use your fourth finger or open string as indicated, to place your string crossings conveniently on the beat.

In section B, bar two, the open E *pedal tones* facilitate the following *shifts* to third, then fifth *position.* Be sure to land on these positions with a raised second finger.

In section C, bar three, land on third position B♯ with a raised second finger. In bar four shift back only a half step to second position. Stay there until bar 10.

Pay particular attention to the *trills* in bars 3, 7, and 11 of this section. Slow practice with a metronome, and a good accent on that downbow will help nail this syncopation. Play that note short and use sufficient bow on the following quarter note to return you to your optimum *sautillé* spot in the bow.

The section D melody is played entirely *sul G,* shifting as indicated between first, second, third, and fifth positions. Note the expressive *slides* in bars 12, 18, and 22. Another melody instrument can play the little answers at the end of each phrase.

After the transitional C♯7 trill, pick up the *reprise* even faster!

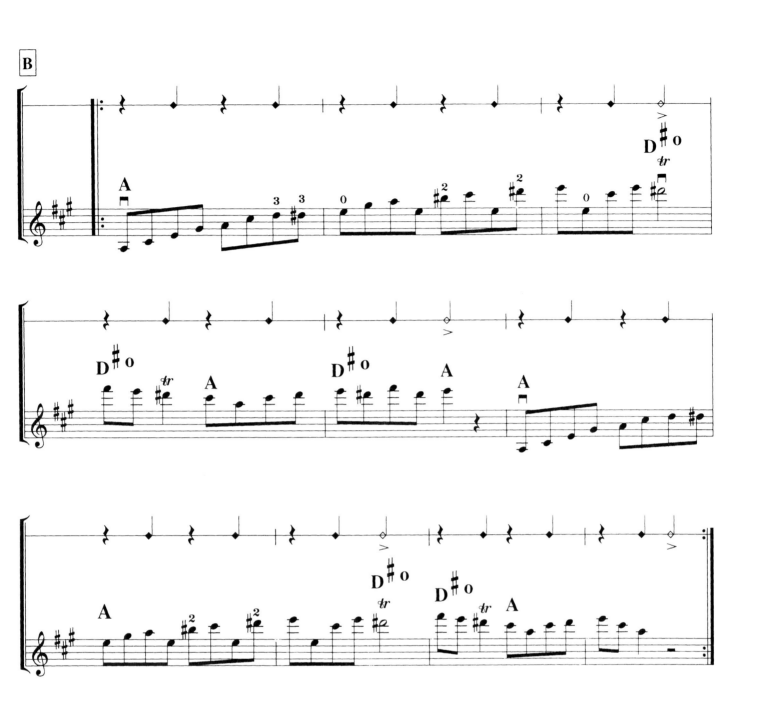

53

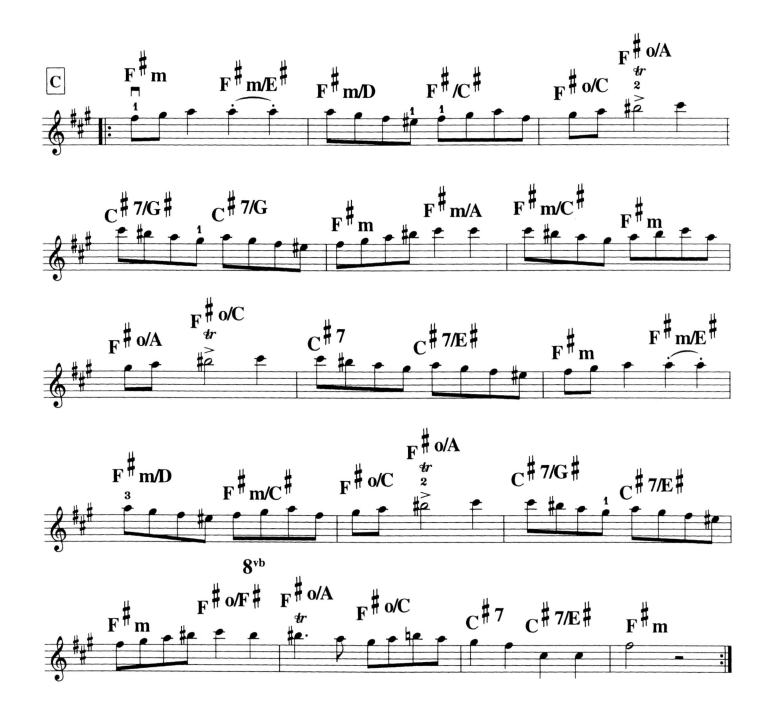

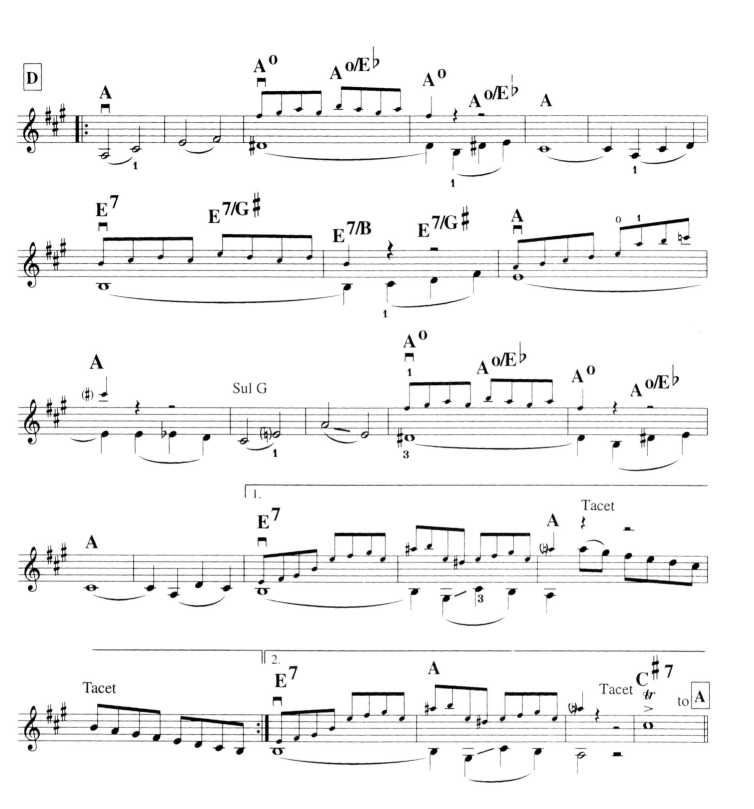

E Minor-Hungarian Medley

The Old Gypsy

The ***contrary motion*** in the ***walking bass line*** in sections C and C´, ***upbow staccato chromatic glissando*** near the end and several varieties of expressive ***slides*** throughout, give this Hungarian standard "A Vén Cigány", polish and enduring appeal. The ***portamento*** in bar three ascends from the starting note of the ***shift,*** whereas the first one in bar 15 slides into the target note. The second one in bar 15 (in the reverse direction) combines both types. Bar three's Am6 is replaced with F#° on its repeat in bar seven.

56

Swallows Flying

Each section of this selection "Repül a Szán" **accelerates** from a deliberate beginning (with **walking bass lines**) to **friss** tempo by bar eight of that section. The accompaniment begins with a lyric **táragató** or clarinet line, changing to harmony and finally **kontra** rhythm.

Hungarian Gypsy Practice Tune

The Rajko School Song

This is the warm-up number for the **Rajko** (pronounced "Roy´-ko") Hungarian Gypsy children's orchestra, a state institution founded to foster and encourage a national treasure! It's an exercise with two **harmonies,** in miniature Hungarian song form (the second phrase repeating the first a fifth higher). The B section opens with the standard Gypsy chord progression IV-I-V-I.

Play ABB; then repeat AB´B´ indefinitely. This format gives optimum benefit of the finger-twisting B´ variation, a workout on sequential repetitions of the Gypsy repertoire's "standard lick." The first and second violins (if there is no third violin) can substitute the open A string for the first note of bars one through four of section B´.

Start out **medium** tempo or slower and gradually increase speed until you drop! Use the basic **primás** bowstroke (*see* "The Gypsy Touch") for A, **legato** bowing for B and, once your speed allows, **sautillé** on B´.

The Rajko Song

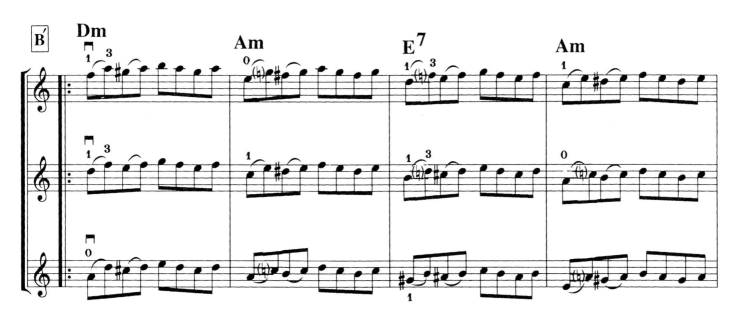

or:

A Minor-Hungarian Medley #1

The Loveliest Girl in the World

This simple *csárdás* medley begins with a folk song rather than a *hallgató*. This opener, "Csak egy Kislány van a Világon," gained fame as the interlude in Sarasate's "Zigeunerweisen." Gypsy embellishments include the F♯° at the end of bar eight, and the *8va* variation in the last four bars.

The Cottage with the Green Window Frames

Play this **verbunk,** "Zöldablakos Kicsi Ház," with a little give-and-take to the melodic rhythm.

March tempo

Go Ahead Bug, Sting Me!

In this *friss* "Csipd Meg, Bogar!," "sting" the accented notes. The trill on the third finger high C in bar six of the B section can be executed with the second finger, B. **Bass** and **rhythm** hold one long note per two bars on all the A sections. Bass players can **walk** the bass lines up or down on the E7 chords.

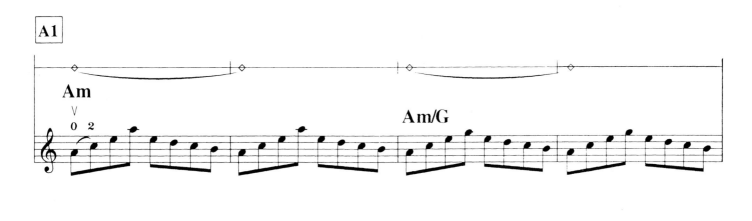

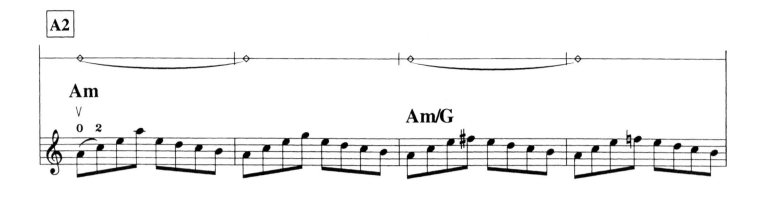

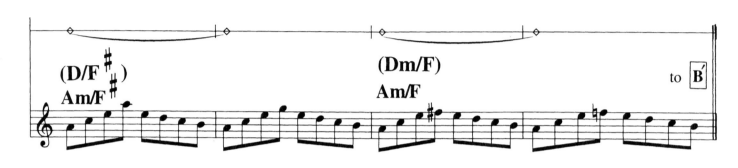

Beautiful Rose

We arranged this *friss* "Szép a Rózsám," as a duet. If you play it twice, both violins can play section A *pizzicato* the second time around. Note the **contrary motion** in bars two and five of the B and B′ parts, and the melody's accented D♯ *tritone* over the A° in the 10th bars of those sections.

Fast

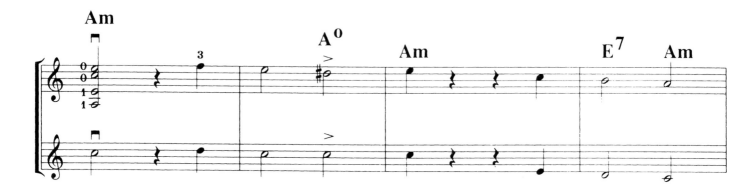

C Major/C Minor/A Minor-
Hungarian Medley

Beautiful Blue Eyes

Dispensing with the *hallgató,* this set of Hungarian Gypsy renditions kicks off with two popular Hungarian drinking songs, starting with this *verbunk* "Aza Szép".

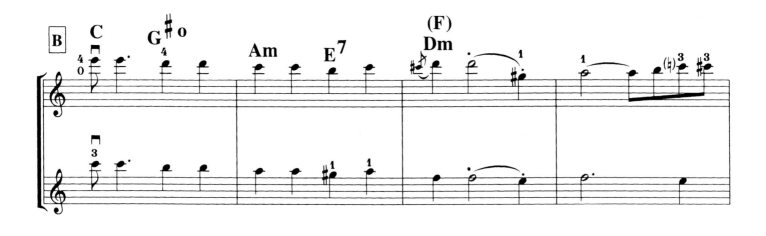

Hey Delade

Pick up the tempo and switch to *friss bass* and *rhythm* patterns.

Dobra Dobra

The *bass* plays whole notes on the first four bars of A and A´. Note the *bass* and *rhythm section* stops at the beginning of sections B and B´.

Mezöségi Hora

This final *friss* is an instrumental dance from the Hungarian-speaking Mezöség region of Transylvania. The second violin switches from **harmony** to **kontra** for this last tune. The A melody can be played under B by another instrument.

C Major Friss

Another instrument can *improvise* eighth note lines over this melody. The *bass* can *walk* up or down from G7 to C on the first and second endings.

D-Hungarian Medley

Your Red Polka Dot Dress

This medley shows examples of **kontra,** beginning with this **hallgató** "Piros Pettyes Ruháskadban."

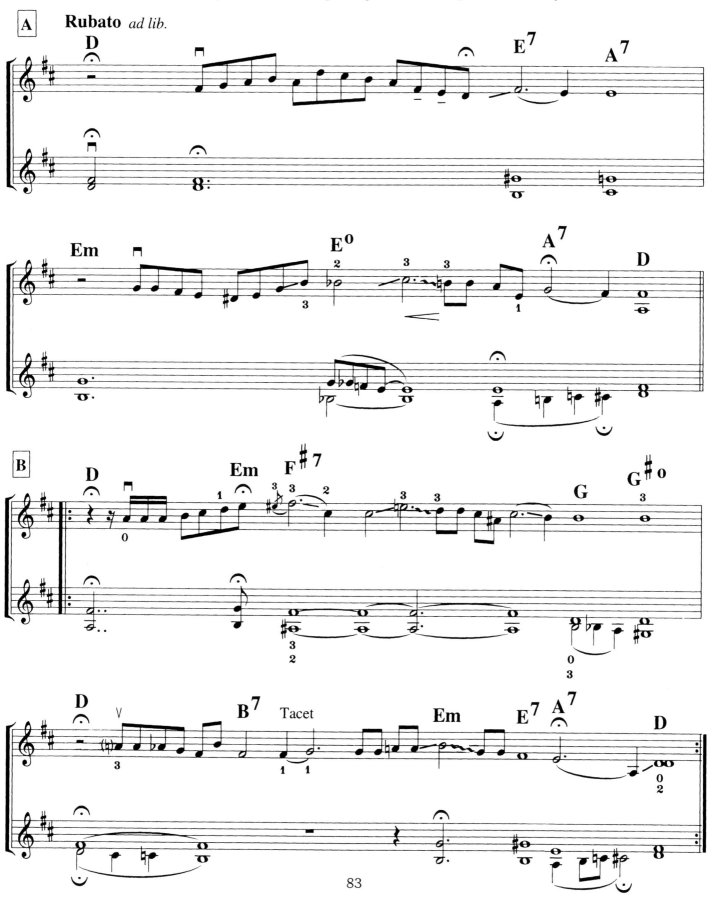

The Wheat and Barley are Scarce

This **verbunk** "Ritka Búza, Ritka Árpa" uses both **dotted** rhythms typical of Hungarian music.

Casino Csárdás

This *friss* "Kaszinó Csárdás" displays three different **kontra** strokes: plain **offbeat**, syncopated, and four-to-a-bow. In section D, contrast is created by the **ad lib.** question and answer phrases, and the **bass** and **rhythm** held notes. The **bass** plays whole notes in bars one through four of that section.

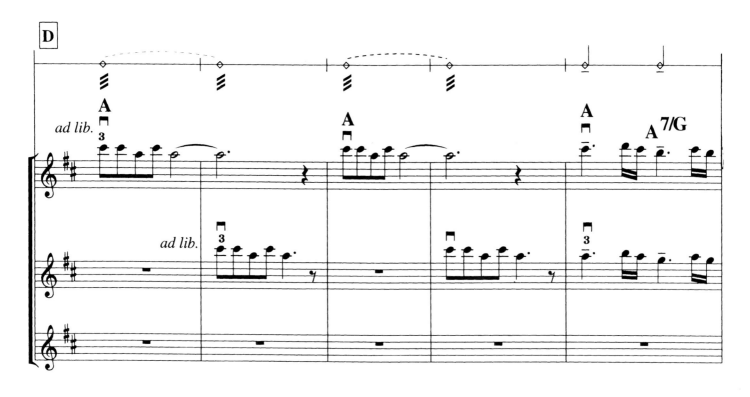

D Minor/D Major-Hungarian Tunes

Abandoned

Section B's tonally rich descending double-stop progression in this quintessential Hungarian lament "Elhagyatva" can elicit tears. Use the **slide with a shake** liberally. You can **ritard** the **upbow staccato** at the end of A´, changing it into a **flying staccato** and then a **flying spiccato,** for added emphasis.

Abandoned

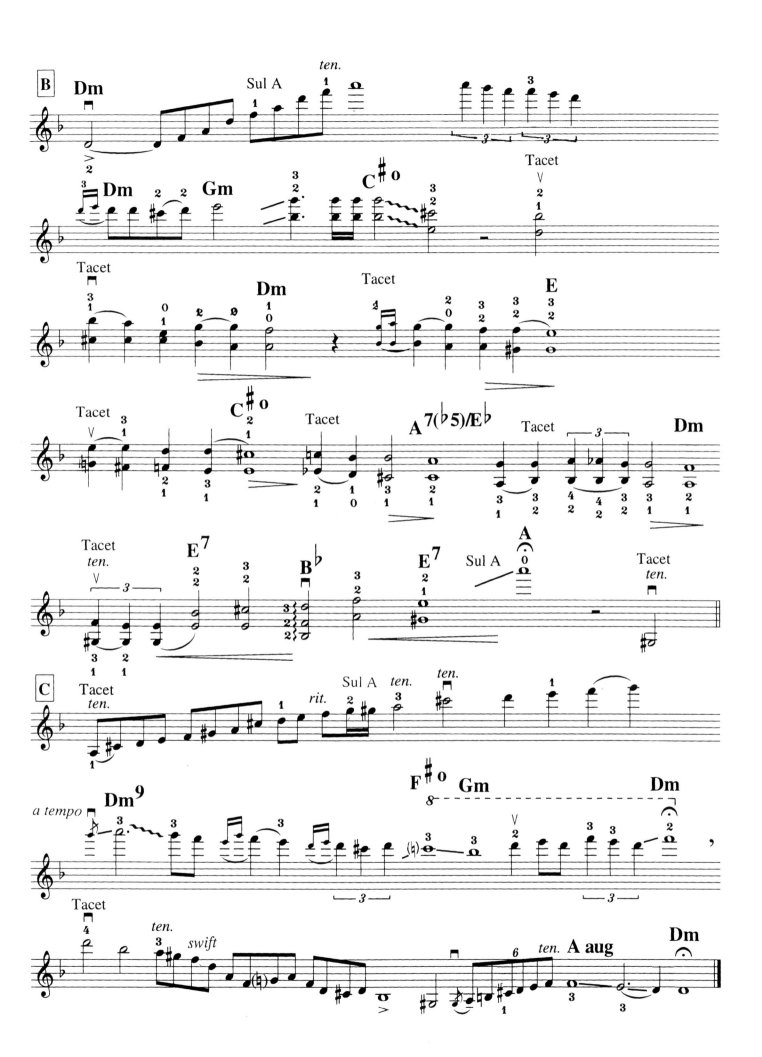

Clarinet Csárdás

One of the most popular selections in the Hungarian Gypsy repertoire, the "Klarinét Csárdás" has countless variations. Start slow and gradually pick up speed. The **rhythm section** stops in the **reprise** add variety.

Variation 1

Alternate Variation 1

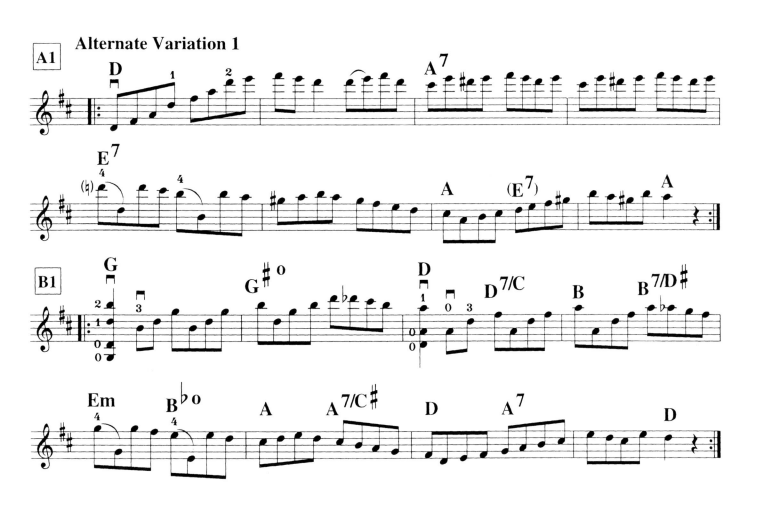

Variation 2

A Minor-Hungarian Medley #2

If You Love Me, Never Leave

The poignant *hallgató* "Fa Leszek, ha Fának vagy Virága" is arranged here as a duet. Artificial *harmonics* embellish section C.

No More Blondes for Me

The graceful opening of this tune "Nem Kell a Szöke" embellishes the actual theme (stated in bars 9-10 + one beat). You can start deliberately and increase speed to a little faster than *medium tempo* by bar nine. The lead or rhythm can show off by *arpeggiating* the A° *chord* near the end of sections B and B´, followed by a pregnant pause while the violin plays the ensuing three pickup notes.

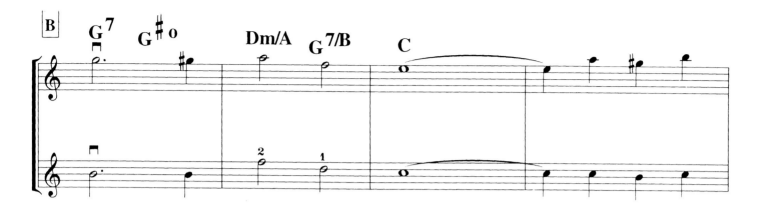

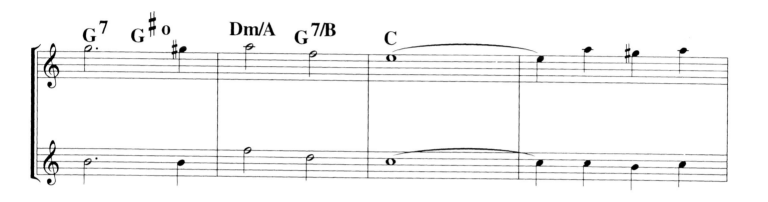

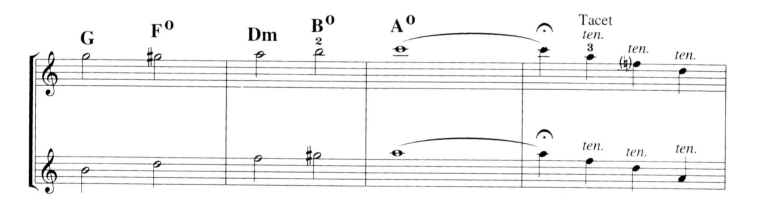

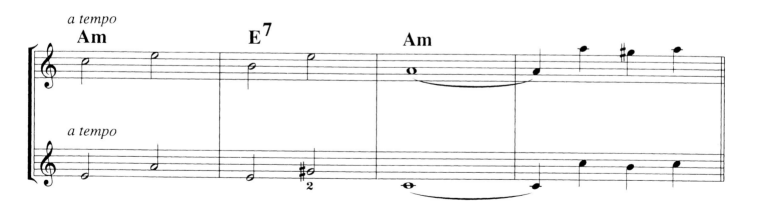

101

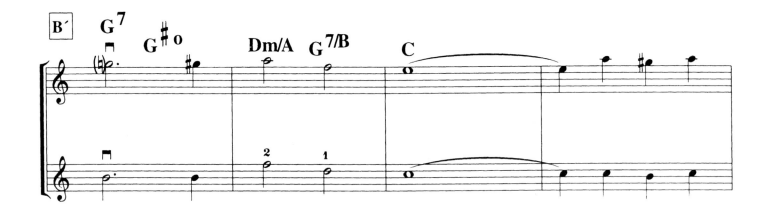

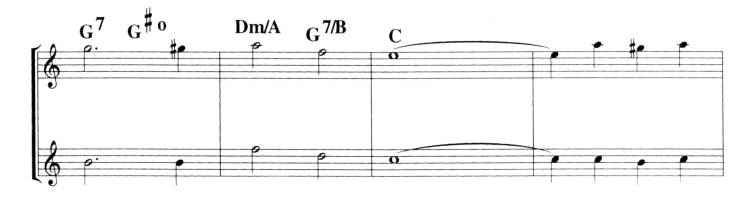

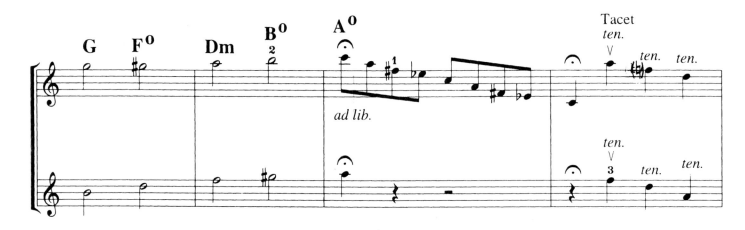

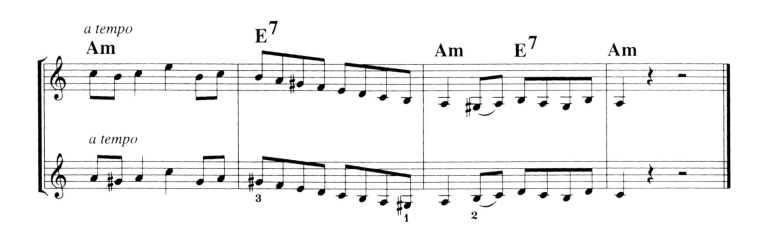

Szüreti Dance

Here are three choruses of "Szüreti Tánc" so you can get a feel for repeating a tune several times. The first eight bars of A2 in this *friss* are similar to those of B2 in "Invitation to Dance" (A Minor-Hungarian Medley #3). Play bars one through two and five through six of section B4 using the *portato* bowstroke. **Bass** plays the first eight bars of all the B sections with that same stroke.

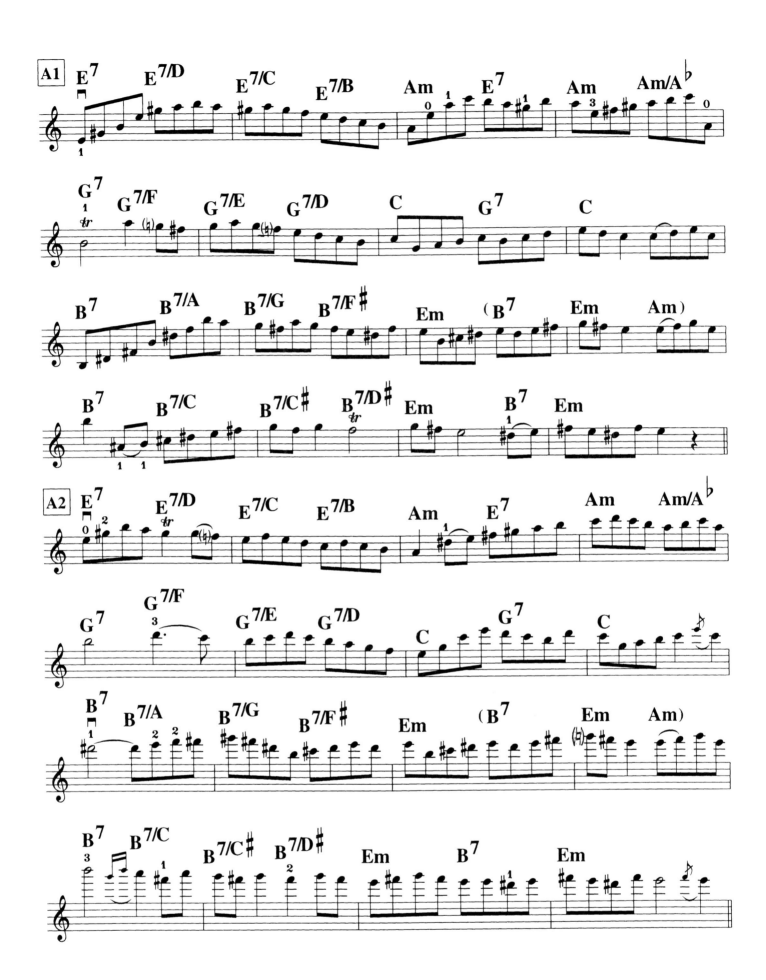

A Minor-Hungarian Medley #3

Gloomy Sunday

Billie Holiday introduced this Hungarian "suicide song," "Somoru Vasharnop" to American audiences before the Second World War. We favor this version for its **walking bass line,** and its plunge to a chilling B♭ **tritone** over the **dominant chord** before the final resolution. Gypsies vary the tune by playing it in the E string stratosphere, in fingered harmonics or in double stops. Be creative!

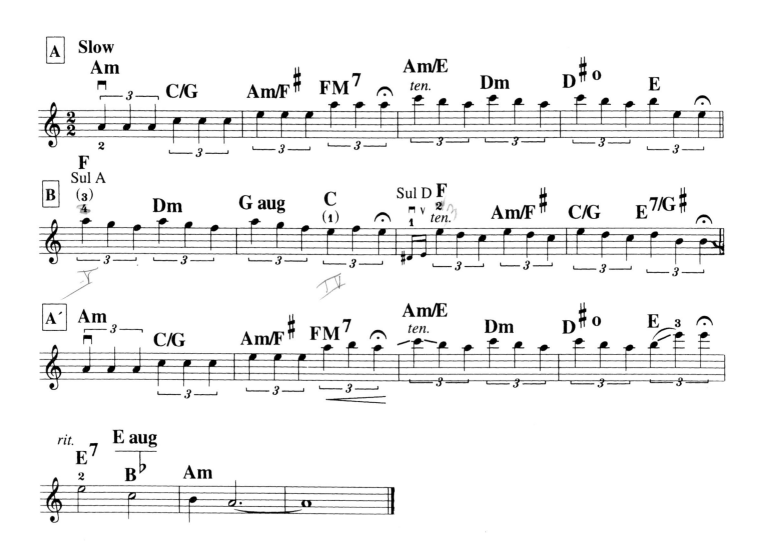

The Horse's Head Can Handle My Sorrow

The title "Nagy a Feje, Búscúlon a Ló" refers to the composer's horse, whose large head, already hanging down, seems much more capable of carrying his troubles than his own.

Invitation to Dance

We present a full three-chorus version of this showy *friss* "Most Kezdödik a Tánc" as an example of varying a piece over several repetitions. The swooping, soaring variation covers a wide range, contrasting melodic register and direction. The first eight bars of section B2 are similar to those of A2 in "Szüreti Tánc" (A Minor-Hungarian Medley #2). The **ghost note** open E's in A and A´ facilitate **shifting**. The trilled C's in section B can be executed with the lower neighbor, B.

110

Hungarian Kesergö

Bihari Kesergö

The Gypsy composer János Bihari travelled and played in Hungary in the early 1800's. One Gypsy violinist I knew used this showpiece, which *he* called "Csermák" (pronounced "Cher´-mak"), after the Gypsy composer Antal Csermák (1774?-1822), for his daily warm-up. It's a good representation of the various techniques and textures you'll find throughout the **Gypsy violin** repertoire.

The timing in the rich double stop *ad lib* introduction is extremely flexible, as you can hear on the companion recording. This **legato solo** section segues with a long, contrasting upbow *flying staccato/spiccato* and harmonic, to the **sul G** leap opening the **hallgató**. The contrast of the A major/F♯ minor **keys** in the **hallgató** (A and B sections) is echoed, after the **verbunk's** varied open E **pedal tone** display, in the final *friss*. *Ricochet* the pickup to the *friss* (section D); drop the bow on the string from the air.

112

114

118

*"The Gypsy artist is one who takes the theme of a song or dance, just like the text of a discussion, as a poetic memorial, and who moves and flutters round this notion, of which he never loses sight, in the course of his **improvisation.** Most admired of all is one who lavishly enriches his own subject with runs, appoggiaturas, leaps, tremolos, chord stopping, diatonic and chromatic scales..."*

—Franz List

G Minor-Hungarian Medley

The Forest is Even Prettier in the Fall

We thank Monitor Records for permission to use Hungarian Gypsy Bela Babai's version of this ***csárdás*** format set, replete with expressive ***slides,*** fingerings, and bowings. This first number "Szép az Erdö Öszel is Szép" uses the old Hungarian song form where the second phrase repeats the first a fourth or fifth higher.

Your Blue Eyes are Stunning

Play this middle tune "Jaj de Két Szép Szeme van Máganak" with a little **rubato**. **Bass** and **rhythm** play one downbeat and one offbeat respectively, to the bar, except as noted.

(2)

Heavenly Csárdás

You may recognize the theme of this "Istenes Csárdás" popularized by Brahms in his "Hungarian Dance #1." Start this tune slowly, *accelerating* to a moderate *friss* tempo by bar 15 of A. From there you can continue speeding up, to a frenzy at B. (You can also then break tempo and start B, with its opening *portato* bowing, *deliberately* and *accelerate* to its fifth bar.)

Quick Reference Key

○   is often played ○⊂ *(see **crescendo**).*

♩, ♩   are generally played ♩, ♩ in medium to fast tempo tunes. Combine the ***detaché porté*** with the ***semi-staccato*** for the basic ***prímás*** bowstroke.

♫♫   can be played ♫♫ (***spiccato*** or ***sautillé***), particularly in a ***friss.***

♫♫   ***Spiccato*** or ***sautillé***

♩   ***Staccato***

♩   ***Semi-staccato***

♩   1) ***Detaché porté;*** 2) Brush stroke (can also be slurred).

♩♩, ♩♩♩♩   ***Portato.*** (Standard bowings for ***bass*** and ***kontra.***)

𝄾 ♩ 𝄾 ♩   Standard ***kontra offbeat*** bowing.

♩ ♩   Slurred notes with a break between them created by stopping, or bouncing the bow. Sometimes used for compensatory bowing, to reverse direction.

♩♩♩♩♩♩   ***Staccato, flying staccato,*** or ***flying spiccato.*** Used as a flourish in ***cadenzas.***

♫♩   ***Ricochet***

♫♩   Small notes with stems reversed indicate a line played by another instrument.

♫♫   ***Extended beam.*** Keep repeating the included notes ***ad lib.***

◇, ◇, ◇   Diamond head notes above the staff indicate rhythm variants to be played by the ***rhythm section,*** and ***bass*** where appropriate.

♫, ♪   ***Grace notes***

(♩)   ***Ghost note***

(♮) (♭) (♯)   ***Courtesy accidental***

↑ ↓   Play the note somewhat flat or sharp.

Left-hand pizzicato

Broken chord

\ , / *Slide* in the direction indicated.

Slide with a shake

> *Accent*

Crescendo

Decrescendo

, Used here to indicate lift the bow (and usually retake it in the same direction).

// *Cutoff*

Fermata

[A] *Rehearsal letter* indicating a main section.

[A´] *Rehearsal letter* indicating a variation of the designated section.

[A1] *Rehearsal letter* indicating one of multiple variations of a section.

⊕ *Coda*

Glossary

8va. an octave higher.

8vb. an octave lower.

Accel. Accelerando. Steadily accelerate the tempo.

Accent (>). Use bow speed and a forefinger "bite" to achieve this effect.

Ad lib. *Ad libitum* "at pleasure." You are free to interpret this passage as you please.

Arpeggiate. Play the notes of a *chord* in sequence, one note at a time, (reversing direction if desired). An arpeggio can span from several notes to several octaves.

A tempo. Resume previous tempo.

Augmented (aug). A *dominant* chord with a raised fifth.

Bass. In the Gypsy ensemble it is typically a bowed upright string bass. Players generally use the German bow hold.

On slow and *rubato* numbers it holds sustained tones with the *kontra,* either *legato* or *tremolo.*

On march tempo (*verbunk*) pieces it bows on the beat with the *kontra* two or four half notes to the bow, using the *detaché porté* or *portato* bowing. (*See* "The Wheat and Barley are Scarce" for an example.)

On *medium tempo* and *fast* pieces, it usually plays quarter notes on the beat, *detaché porté,* alternating with the *kontra's offbeat.* This can be varied with the quarter note two- or four-to-a-bow *portato* bowing, especially on *walking bass lines.* (*See* "Casino Csárdás" for an example.)

Broken chord ({). Start the *chord* on the lower strings, then cross to the upper ones.

Cadenza. A flashy show-off section for the violin.

Changes. *Chords* in the progression played by the *rhythm section.* Changes are indicated in this book above the melody line. A number after a chord indicates the inclusion of that scale degree.

Chord. Two or more notes played simultaneously. (*See changes, broken chord.*)

Chromatic. By half steps.

Chromatic glissando. A succession of chromatic notes played in *glissando.* Play it with the pad of single finger, stopping intermittently to articulate each pitch as you open the forearm to move down the fingerboard (or vice-versa). Often combined with the *upbow* or *downbow staccato.*

Cimbalom (pronounced "cheem´-ba-lohm"). Like a large hammered dulcimer, it plays both lead and accompaniment in the Gypsy ensemble.

Coda (⊕). A tag after the end of a song. If you see the two coda symbols, jump from the first to the second the last time through, to end the song.

The standard coda at the end of a *csárdás* medley is the *chords* **IV-V-I,** everyone playing on the beat. An example is written out in "Bessarabian Girl." You can end any fast song with a similar coda.

Colla parte. Follow the lead, particularly with regard to tempo nuances.

Contrary motion. An alternative to parallel *harmony;* the harmony moves in the opposite direction from the melody. This can also apply to *bass* and *rhythm.*

Courtesy accidental (♮), (♭), or (♯). A natural, flat, or sharp placed in parenthesis as a reminder to resume playing that pitch as indicated by the key signature.

Crescendo (⊂———). The Gypsy crescendo is especially effective on a long note of a *hallgató* or the *doina* section of a Romanian *hora.* Use an upbow if possible, conserving the bow at the beginning of the stroke; then speed up the bow to maximize dynamic power as you approach the frog.

Csárdás (pronounced "char´-dahsh"). 1) The Hungarian popular song group and Gypsy medley form, named after the roadside inns hosting Hungary's famous couple dance by the same name. Its three sections, *hallgató, verbunk,* and *friss,* progress from slow, medium to fast respectively. Most of the Hungarian medleys in this volume follow the Csárdás format. 2) A *friss.*

Cutoff (//). "Train tracks." Stop abruptly.

D.C. Da capo "from the head." Take it again from the top.

Decrescendo (———⊃). Decrease volume. (*See* also *crescendo.*)

Deliberate. *Medium tempo* or less, with emphasis.

Detaché porté (♩). Stress the beginning of each note with increased speed and a slight forefinger nudge; then release. This is sometimes accompanied by a broadening of the tempo. The *bass* and *kontra* often employ this stroke. (*See* also *portato.*)

Diatonic. Scale-wise.

Diminished (°). A chord (or portion thereof), comprised of four intervals of a minor third.

Doina. A wailing Romanian lament stressing repeated notes, functionally similar to the Hungarian *hallgató.* We've included it in its popular accelerated and abbreviated form as an interlude in fast numbers.

Dominant (e.g., E7). The V7 chord. It resolves to the root, or I chord.

Dotted. ♪♩ is sometimes interpreted as ♪.♪ or ♪♪. and ♩ ♩ sometimes as ♩. ♪ or ♪ ♩.. The latter rhythms derive from the Hungarian language.

Double, triple, and **quadruple stops.** Two or more notes played simultaneously. They can be used to fatten the sound in the melody, or to create a rhythm part (*see kontra*), and can be *improvised* using your harmonic ear and knowledge.

Downbow staccato (♩♩♩♩♩). A group of notes played *staccato,* on one downbow. (*See* also *flying staccato, flying spiccato.*)

Fast. Here refers to *friss* tempo (half note = 120-200) and style.

Fermata (⌒). "Bird's eye." Hold the note.

Fine. The end. If you see this in the middle of a song, keep going and end at this point when the song repeats.

Flying staccato (♪♪♪♪♪♪). A series of notes taken on one bow, skipping the bow slightly between them and attacking each with a slight forefinger pinch. (*See* also *flying spiccato, ricochet.*)

Flying spiccato (♪♪♪♪♪♪). A series of notes taken on one bow, bouncing the bow between them and attacking each with a slight forefinger pinch. (*See* also *flying staccato, ricochet.*)

Fraigish. Probably the most popular *Klezmer* scale. It's the *harmonic minor* in the *key* of the song, starting on its fifth scale degree and played over the *dominant* chord.

Friss. "Fresh." A Hungarian fast number in cut time (half note = mm 120-200). The final section of a *csárdás* medley. It often starts out slow, accelerating deliberately to *friss* tempo in the first eight-sixteen bars. It can continue to accelerate from there to the end. The general rule of thumb is to play the *friss* as fast as you can, *spiccato* or *sautillé.*

The standard *friss bass/kontra* rhythm is ♪ ♩ ♪ ♩ (*See* "Casino Csárdás" for an example.) In general, *frisses* end with a *coda* (*see*). In a coda and in sections punctuated by rhythmic stops, everyone plays his part of the *chord* on the beat.

Ghost note (♩). Play the note so rapidly and lightly as to be barely audible. Ghost notes are sometimes used to reverse the bowing or facilitate *shifts,* or as ornaments.

Glissando (＼ , ／). A *slide* spanning a large interval. (*See* also *chromatic glissando.*)

Grace note (♪). A very quick note (often found in pairs or groups) preceding and usually connected to the main note. You can play grace notes in Gypsy music like *trills,* by widening the *vibrato* and/or throwing the entire hand forward from the (somewhat collapsed) wrist.

For our purposes here, you can execute a grace note with any finger above the main note. For example: a note played by the first finger is often ornamented by tapping the third or even the fourth finger.

Gypsy violin. The playing style of *Gypsy violinists,* which has evolved from entertainment at *slavas* to commercial performances and recordings sold worldwide. Characterized by its adaptation of the surrounding culture's repertoire to its expressive style, it is most acclaimed in its urban Hungarian form.

Gypsy violinists. A Gypsy who plays the above-mentioned style. Major current and recent artists play on recordings and in restaurants of large cities. They include members of Balogh, Horvath, Lakatos, Mirando, and Nemeth families.

Hallgató. A soulful, *rubato* slow number, often the first in a *csárdás* medley. Long notes are stretched, with a concurrent *crescendo* and intensification of *vibrato.* They are contrasted with swift connecting passages of short notes played with tiny strokes.

The accompanying instruments hold long *chords,* the *kontra* sometimes preceding the *changes* with a string of quick chromatic or diatonic passing tones. (See "Your Red Polka Dot Dress" for an example.)

Harmonic (♩ , ♩). 1) Natural harmonic: a fractional node on a string which, when touched lightly, produces an upper partial of its fundamental pitch. 2) Artificial harmonic: a fingered harmonic, which can be produced for any note by putting the first or second finger on that note, and simultaneously lightly touching the note a fourth or fifth above, to produce a pitch two octaves or an octave and a fifth respectively, higher.

Playing a melody, or portion thereof, in harmonics, is a favorite Gypsy variation.

Harmonic minor. Natural minor scale with a raised seventh degree, creating an interval of minor third between the sixth and seventh degrees, and a half step from the seventh to the tonic. (*See* also *melodic minor.*) These intervals give Gypsy music much of its harmonic flavor.

Harmony. The first harmony typically follows the lead in generally parallel motion a third or sixth below, conforming harmonically to *chord* and passing tones. Chord alterations are sometimes used, especially to maintain a consistent interval between the two voices. A second harmony would follow suit below the first. The resultant occurrences of parallel fourth or fifths may sound new to you, as classical composers usually took great pains to avoid this type of *voice-leading;* however, it is idiomatic to this folk style.

126

Other options include: 1) *contrary motion;* 2) playing the harmony above the melody, or; 3) sustained notes. The harmony player sometimes switches intervals (e.g., from a third to a sixth) between his part and the adjacent one for more consonance.

Harmony parts can require advanced technique (to fit the melody intervallically) and an experienced ear. Novices are often showcased on the melody, while more seasoned players handle the backup. We've included a few examples of harmony (among them the C/C Minor/A Minor Hungarian Medley) as well as *kontra,* and invite you to create your own.

Hora. A broad term encompassing many Eastern European dance types. Here it refers to either a *joc* or a *fast* Romanian circle dance. Play the fast hora as you would a *friss.* Romanian tunes, including this type, often have an odd number of measures in one or more phrases.

Improvisation. Varying a selection by substituting one's own notes, *chords,* expressive devices or arrangements. The Gypsy style is highly improvisatory and the material herein represents examples and suggestions only.

Joc. Refers here to a slow hora in three, originating in Romania and popularized by *Klezmer* musicians. The dotted half note equals about mm 40. Not to confuse it with the waltz, the *bass* and *rhythm section* play only on beats one and three.

Kesergö. A concert piece in *csárdás* format, progressing from slow to fast.

Key. The tonality of a piece, governed by the major or minor scale upon which it is based. Gypsy music is created for the violin by violinists, to lie naturally under the fingers and bow. Tunes are typically rendered in those keys corresponding to the open strings, and their relative minors (G/Em, D/Bm, A/F♯m, E).

Klezmer. Jewish/Yiddish music of Eastern Europe.

Kontra. Part or all of the rhythm section of the Gypsy ensemble. These musicians play double stops, mostly on the two lower strings of the violin, or on the viola. The player turns his instrument sideways as much as 90° to facilitate this, supporting its neck on the inside of the left wrist and resting his chin on its side.

On slow and *rubato* pieces the kontra holds sustained *chords,* either *legato* or *tremolo.* An example is written out in "Your Red Polka Dot Dress." It sometimes precedes the *changes* with a string of quick chromatic or diatonic passing tones.

For *march* (*verbunk*) tempo pieces, it joins the bass, connecting two or four half notes to a bow on the beat using the *portato* bowing. (*See* "The Wheat and Barley are Scarce" for an example.)

On *medium tempo* and *fast* pieces, it usually plays *offbeat* quarter notes. (Exceptions include codas, and sections punctuated by rhythmic stops where it plays on the beat with the bass.) This can be varied (particularly when simulating a *walking bass line*) with the quarter note four-to-a-bow *portato* bowing. (*See* "Casino Csárdás," for an example.)

The *kontra* pinch hits for the *bass* if none is available, using the same bowing and playing the bass notes within its usual double-stop progression.

Leading tone. A half step below a chord tone; e.g., the seventh degree of a major scale, which resolves to the tonic.

Left-hand pizzicato ( ). Pluck the string with the left hand.

Legato. Smooth, sustained bowing.

Major 7th (M⁷). A major chord in which the seventh degree is included.

March tempo. *See verbunk.*

Medium tempo. Here means half note = mm 70-110 or so in cut time.

Melodic minor. Minor scale with the sixth and seventh degrees raised on the ascent and lowered on the descent. (*See* also *harmonic minor.*)

Naturale. Resume playing without the preceding special effect(s).

Offbeat (𝄽 ♩ 𝄽 ♩). A *kontra* rhythm, particularly for *fast* passages, alternating with the bass notes played on the beat.

Move the bow back and forth, between only the first two to six inches from the frog, by swiftly bending and flexing your fingers. Release, barely leaving the string, after every stroke, allowing the notes to resonate. Keep your right wrist and fingers loose. The bow hair may turn outward.

Pedal tone. A repeated tone, alternating with other notes. (*See* "Whistling Hora" and "Bihari Kesergö".) Gypsy violinists often use open strings as pedal tones, as a *shifting* device.

Pizz. Pizzicato. Pluck the string (*See* also *left-hand pizzicato.*)

Portamento. "Carrying" the sound from one note to the next. An expressive slide during a shift. Can be done: 1) from the starting note; 2) into the target note, or; 3) both. (*See* "The Old Gypsy.")

Portato (♩ ♩ ♩ ♩). Like the *detaché porté,* except that two or more notes are taken in one bow. In such a series of connected notes, nudge the beginning of each with the forefinger, stressing it with increased speed, then release. Primarily a *kontra* and *bass* bowing.

Positions. These expedite navigating the instrument. Gypsy violinists use half position and the even numbered positions as well as the more familiar odd numbered ones. (*See* also *shifts.*)

Prímás (pronounced "pree´-mahsh"). The lead violinist and spokesman of a Gypsy ensemble.

Rall. Rallentando. Slow down gradually.

Rehearsal letters (𝐀). These divide the piece into sections to facilitate finding your place.

Replacement fingerings (♩ ♩). Use different fingers for adjacent repetition(s) of a note. This gives the note an expressive articulation.

Reprise. Recapitulation of the opening section of a number.

Rhythm section. The *kontra* (*See* for a discussion of what to play) and/or any other rhythm instruments in the ensemble such as guitar, accordion, piano, or *cimbalom.*

Ricochet (♫♪). "Throw" the bow, so it bounces for two or more successive notes taken in one stroke. (*See flying staccato, flying spiccato.*)

Rit. Ritardando. Slow down.

Rom. Romani, or Gypsy people, who migrated from northern India, spreading throughout Europe and Eastern Europe.

Romanian minor. Harmonic minor with a raised fourth (a *tritone* from the root), creating a total of two minor thirds and four half steps in the scale. Romanians use many variants of this scale in their music.

Rubato. Stretch the long notes and quicken the short ones. Used predominantly in the *hallgató.* (See "Your Red Polka Dot Dress" for an example.)

Sautillé (♩♩♩♩). Springing bow. Bounce the stick, keeping the hair in contact with the string.

Semi-staccato (♩). Separate the notes, in the same manner as *staccato,* but with less punctuation.

Sempre. "Always," "still." Keep doing [the previous instruction].

Shifts can be accomplished in several ways in addition to the standard shift: by *portamento,* by *replacement fingerings,* and by interspersing an open string as a ghost note or *pedal tone* while shifting. Half step shifts are sometimes used. (*See* also *positions.*)

Simile. Continue playing in the same manner.

Slava. A Gypsy feast for a saint's day wedding or other festivity. Funerals are also important social functions. *Rom* travel across entire countries to congregate at such events, celebrating or grieving with abandon. Their music, essential to these gatherings, exudes life and love.

Slides ($\searrow$, $\nearrow$). Range from barely perceptible to very drawn out, particularly when leading to certain long notes. In the latter case, you can "sit on" the starting note of the slide with no inflection, before commencing up or down the string, gradually increasing the speed of the slide, intensity of *vibrato* and bow speed for a *crescendo* as you approach the target note.

Slides between two notes can be done with the starting note finger, the target note finger, or both. You can often slide into a note preceded by a rest. A note followed by a rest can sometimes end with a downward slide. (*See* also: *glissando, chromatic glissando, portamento,* and *slide with a shake.*)

Slide with a shake ($\searrow$, $\nearrow$). Shake your whole hand to create a wide vibrato while sliding. (*See* "Abandoned.")

Solo. 1) Unaccompanied or with minimal accompaniment. 2) Without harmony part.

Spiccato (♪♪♪♪). Bounce the bow anywhere from the balance point (six to eight inches from the frog) to the upper half of the bow, depending on speed and volume. (*See* also *flying spiccato.*)

Staccato (♩). Separate the notes by stopping the bow on the string between them. (*See* also: *semi-staccato, upbow staccato,* and *downbow staccato.*)

Sul G, D, A, or E. On the [G, D, A, or E] string. Used for richer timbre, or for ease of fingering.

Sul ponticello. "At the bridge." Play near the bridge for a whistling sound.

Tacet. No *chord.* Rhythm and bass silent.

Táragató. A hybrid of the clarinet and oboe, often found in Hungarian Gypsy ensembles.

Ten. Tenuto. Stress and elongate the note.

Tremolo (⪢). Shake the bow back and forth on the string(s) as fast as possible.

Trill (*tr*). The Gypsy trill differs from the standard classical trill in the following regards:

Standard trill: "Main note" finger anchors to the string while the trilling finger rapidly lifts and strikes independently.

Gypsy trill: Trilling finger anchors to the "main note" finger. With a somewhat collapsed wrist, wave the hand to widen the vibrato. This rocks both fingers back and forth together, bringing the trilling finger into rapid periodic contact with the string, simultaneously producing vibrato and trill for a liquid sound.

A trill can range in length anywhere from two oscillations to the entire duration of a long note. The latter can begin slowly and deliberately with the standard trill, gradually accelerating and widening into the Gypsy trill.

When trilling a note falling on the fourth finger, trill with the third. (Occasionally other fingers execute an inverted trill.)

Tritone. The interval of an augmented fourth (diminished fifth).

Upbow staccato (♪♪♪♪♪♪). A group of notes played *staccato,* on one upbow. (*See* also *flying staccato, flying spiccato.*)

Vamp. *Bass* (on beat) and *rhythm section* (off beat) alone lay down a preparatory rhythm for a lead entrance. (See "Besserabian Girl," for examples.)

Verbunk. a.k.a. "Lassu." A military-style tune in march time (half note = mm 100 or so) patterned after historic army recruiting songs. It is often the middle section of a *csárdás* medley. The default *bass* and *kontra* bowing pattern is two or four half notes to a bow, on the beat, using the *portato* bowing. (*See* "The Wheat and Barley are Scarce" for an example.)

Vibrato. The basic Hungarian Gypsy vibrato is fast and wide. Favor the backswing onto the pad of your finger. Your thumb can even leave the neck. This technique can make lesser quality instruments sound more resonant. The nervous reflex action of the Gypsy vibrato also forms the basis for *grace notes* and *trills.* Remember to vibrato on *harmonics.*

Use this particularly effective vibrato technique on long notes: begin with none at all and then increase intensity by progressing from slow to fast, and narrow to wide or the reverse. (*See* also *crescendo.*) This is a typical Romanian ornament, vibrato being used otherwise sparingly in this style.

Voice-leading. The progression of vertical intervals from one *chord* into the next.

Walking bass line. Progresses diatonically and/or chromatically. Widespread throughout Eastern European music, this technique creates a smooth progression between *chords.* We've written out some examples (e.g., "Swallows Flying.") and invite your bass player to create more. These work particularly well over *dominant* chords lasting two or more bars.

It can walk in half notes in a medium or fast tempo number. It can also walk in half or whole notes over a sustained *chord.* And it can walk repeated quarter notes in pairs or groups of four notes to the bow, using the *portato* bowing.

130

Bibliography

Blom, Eric. *Grove's Dictionary of Music and Musicians.* St. Martin's Press, New York, New York, 1961.

Casey, Betty. *International Folk Dancing U.S.A.* Doubleday & Company, Garden City, New York, 1981.

Galamian, Ivan. *Principles of Violin Playing and Teaching.* Prentice-Hall, Inc., Englewood Cliffs, New Jersey, 1985.

Harbar, M.A. *A Dark Flame Still Burning, Strad Magazine.* Orpheus Publications, Ltd., London, England, May 1993.

Marre, Jerry. Producer/Director, *The Romany Trail* (Video). Harcourt Films, Shanachie Records, Newton, N.J., 1992.

Sárosi, Bálint. *Folk Music-Hungarian Musical Idiom.* Franklin Printing House, Budapest, Hungary, 1986.

Sárosi, Bálint. *Gypsy Music.* Franklin Printing House, Budapest, Hungary, 1978.

Westrup & Harrison. *The New College Encyclopedia of Music.* W.W. Norton & Company. New York, New York, 1976.

About the Author

Mary Ann Harbar apprenticed with native Gypsy violinists after earning her Bachelor's degree and teaching credential in music from the University of Calfornia. For two decades she and her husband Greg Harbar have entertained sophisticated international audiences studded with royalty, heads of state, and stars, with their Houston, TX band, The Gypsies.